PowerPoint Essentials

A Guide for Real-Life Users (Not Technicians!)

PowerPoint Essentials

A Guide for Real-Life Users (Not Technicians!)

By
George W. Rumsey
Computer Resource Center, Inc.
Chicago, Illinois

Microsoft Excel, Microsoft Word, Microsoft PowerPoint, Microsoft Access, Microsoft Lync, and Microsoft Office are trademarks of Microsoft.

Published by
Computer Resource Center, Inc.
1525 East 53rd Street, Suite 902
Chicago, IL 60615
Telephone (773) 955-4455
Email gwrumsey@att.net
Web www.computer-resource.com

PowerPoint Essentials

A Guide for Real-Life Users (Not Technicians!)

Preface

This instructional manual is not an exhaustive guide to Microsoft PowerPoint. Rather, it is a compass, directing you toward key concepts, terms, and commands you need to learn to use PowerPoint effectively and navigate presentations efficiently. It is geared towards users of PowerPoint 2013 or 365, but would also be appropriate for users of 2010.

It also is not intended for a technical audience. I've tried to keep explanations and examples fairly simple and straight-forward, and not speak in "computerese" as much as possible. Forgive my lapses, because it is difficult to avoid.

I hope you find this manual useful. Remember "rule number one": *the only way to learn how to use a computer is to use a computer.*

George

Overview of Presentations

The key term in PowerPoint is "slide"—a slide is your page. Slides can consist of text, charts, free-hand drawings, clip art, videos, and many other elements. A series of slides strung together into one document ("slide show", frequently called a "deck") creates a "presentation."

PowerPoint can be used to generate a number of useful documents, in addition to presentations. PowerPoint 2013 provides you with a series of different "view" and "print" options. "View" commands include these:

- **Normal view**—where you do your work
- **Slide show**—projects the presentation
- **Outline view**—text content without the graphics or all the formatting
- **Slide sorter view**—organizes your slides, let you rearrange them, turn them on or off, and adding timing for display
- **Notes page**—the speaker's notes for use during the presentation
- **Reading view**—a full-screen view without having to run the presentation; useful when you send someone a presentation you want them to read
- **Slide Master view**—global template for formatting and designing slides

- **Handout Master view**—global template for formatting your handouts
- **Notes Master view**—global template for formatting your speaker notes

When you go to File/Print, you'll find fewer choices. You can print:

- Full page slides (1 per page)
- Notes pages
- Outline
- Handouts (with options for 1, 2, 3, 4, 6, or 9 per sheet)

The built-in or default setting in PowerPoint 2013 is that a slide is 13.333 inches by 7.5 inches, landscape. This establishes what is called an "aspect ratio" of 16:9, used by wide-screen projectors. If you wish to do an on-screen presentation with older projectors, you can re-set the aspect ratio to 4:3 (which sets the slides size to 10 by 7.5 inches, and is the setting used by PowerPoint 2010 and earlier versions). These options are located on the "Slide Size" command under Designs. You can switch back and forth between aspect ratios (to avoid "letter-boxing"), and PowerPoint will try to ensure the proper re-fitting of your elements, but be prepared to have to do some cleanup when you switch.

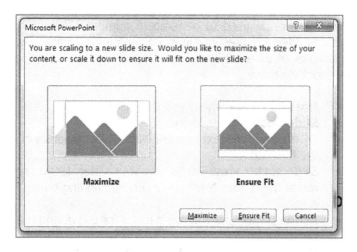

The Screen

The very top of the screen is divided into two parts: the *Quick Access Toolbar* and the *Ribbon*. The top line (upper left corner of your screen) shows you commonly used operations such as *save* and *undo* and *open*. Use the dropdown arrow at the end to add more features.

Below the quick access toolbar is the **Ribbon**, which is divided into "tabs" of choices. The tabs show you "buttons" for various commands, separated into "groups" (such as Font or Paragraph).

To use any feature, click it (once) with the mouse pointer. For example, to turn on bold, point the mouse arrow at the "B" and click the center of it. To turn it off, click the "B" again. Some buttons have "dropdowns" with choices, indicated by a downward pointing arrow (▾); click the arrow for more options. And in the bottom-right corner of some groups, you will find an additional little boxed arrow (▫), which opens a dialog window with more options. At the right end of the ribbon is an up arrow (^) for minimizing (or "collapsing") the ribbon while working.

As you work, if you highlight (select) an area of text, you will see a shadow ribbon appear. This is a shortcut toolbar for commonly used formats. (See page 11 for more examples of and details about screen shortcuts).

At the bottom left of the screen is the status line showing your page number, "theme" (optional to see, turned on or off with the right clicker, indicating your selection of colors, fonts, and effects), and spell check status.

In the lower right corner are "View" buttons for Normal Slide View, Slide Sorter, Reading View, and Slide Show, as well as zoom bars and "fit on screen" commands.

At the bottom center are two additional buttons called Notes and Comments. "Notes" opens and closes the speaker notes window. "Comments" turns on or off any comments embedded in the presentation (you'll find "new comments" on the Review ribbon).

At the right side of the screen is a vertical scroll bar for moving up and down. The scroll bar can be used three different ways. You can click on the up or down arrows (at the top or bottom of the bar) to move line by line; you can pull the box ("elevator") on the bar to go to the top or bottom of the document; or you can click on the blank area to move screen-up or screen-down. At the bottom of the scroll bar are two double-arrows; these are "page up" and "page down" commands for moving an entire slide at a time.

At the left of the screen is a thumbnail view of your slides, useful for quickly moving around, as well as for re-arranging and copying your slides. It can be converted to what is called the "Outline View" by going to the View tab on the Ribbon and clicking Outline View.

Slides, Outlines, and Notes views can be printed. There is an additional print option called "handouts." Handouts do not appear on the screen (only under "Print"), but they allow you to print multiple slides per page for photocopying and distributing to your audience.

Getting Started

When you first open PowerPoint 2013, the screen provides options to do a blank presentation or to create a new presentation from a template design.

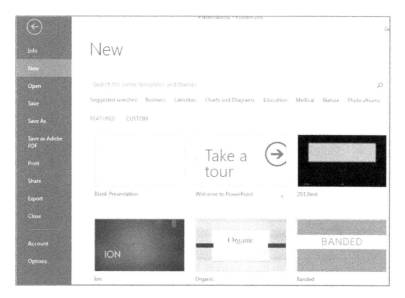

If you select the "blank presentation," you will have the first slide centered on your screen.

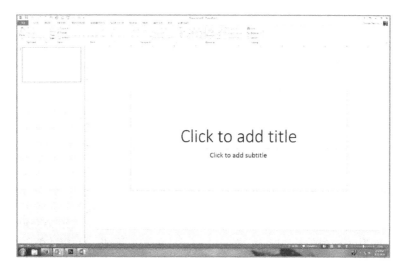

The next step in creating a presentation is deciding what type of "slide" you want, called the slide "layout." PowerPoint provides 9 default layouts:

- Title Slide — Title and subtitle, surrounded by handles which allow you to move and position the content
- Title and Content — Bulleted List, Table, Chart, SmartArt, ClipArt, Picture, or Video.
- Section Header
- Two Content
- Comparison
- Title Only
- Blank
- Content with Caption
- Picture with Caption

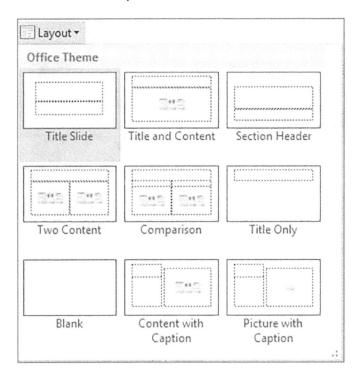

A presentation can contain any combination of these types of slides. Slides are created by clicking the dropdown for "New Slide" on the Home Ribbon, and selecting a layout. If you change your mind, the layout can be switched by the dropdown on the Layout button.

The Ribbon

The Microsoft Office "Ribbon" is separated into categories, which contain subcategories of commands, along with extended pull-down options:

Home

- Clipboard: Cut, Copy, Paste (with Paste Special), Format Painter
- Slides:
  - New Slide—Select from a layout, Duplicate (copy a slide), or Reuse (from other PowerPoint files)
  - Layout—Select or change a layout
  - Reset—Restore default formatting and position
  - Section—Separate parts of a presentation into sections for organization
- Font: Font, Size, Enlarge/Shrink, Clear Formatting, B, I, U, Strikethrough, Shadow, Tighten/Loosen Text, Case, Color
- Paragraph: Bullets, Numbers, Indents, Spacing, Alignment; Text Direction; Text Position within the Textbox; Convert to "SmartArt Graphic"
- Drawing: Autoshapes (long scrolled list), Arrange (Front/Back), Quick Styles, Shape Fill (Textures, Gradients), Shape Outline (Borders and Thickness), Shape Effects (such as "Glow")
- Editing: Find, Replace Select

Insert

- New Slide
- Tables: Insert a Table, Draw a Table, Insert Excel Spread-sheet
- Images
  - Pictures (from files)
  - Online Pictures (clip art)
  - Screenshot
  - Photo Album
- Illustrations
  - Shapes
  - Smart Art
  - Chart
- Apps (purchasable from the Microsoft store)
- Links: Hyperlink, Action (such as "Run Program")
- Comments (sticky notes)

- Text:
  - Text Box: Inserts a text box into the document; the box can be formatted with the "Text Box," which includes text format, box style, shadow effects, 3-D effects, and more.
  - Header & Footer
  - Word Art
  - Date & Time
  - Slide Number
  - Object: A file that exists outside of Word, independent of Word.
- Symbols and equations
- Media: Video, Audio
- Flash

Design

- Themes: Predefined "looks" for your document. Includes options for
  - Colors
  - Fonts
  - Effects.
- Variants
- Customize
  - Slide Size (aspect ratio)
  - Format Background (colors, fills, pictures)

Transitions

- Preview: Test the animation and transition on a particular slide
- Transition to This Slide: Various ways to move from slide to slide during the presentation
- Timing: Apply timing and sound

Animations

- Preview: Test the animation and transition on a particular slide
- Animation: Various ways to move parts of a slide during the presentation
- Advanced Animation: Animation Pane, with various settings and options (such as speed and sound effects)
- Timing

Slide Show

- Start Slide Show: From Beginning, From Current Slide, Present Online, Custom Slide Show
- Set Up: Set Up Slide Show, Hide Slide, Rehearse Timings, Record Slide Show, Play Narrations, use Timings, Show Media Controls
- Monitors: Resolution, Shown on, Use Presenter View

Review

- Proofing
  - Spelling
  - Research: Access to several language tools, such as thesaurus and translation
  - Thesaurus: Synonyms
- Language: Translate, define language
- Comments: New comment, Delete, Go to Previous/Next, Show/Hide Comments
- Compare
- OneNote: Send content to MS OneNote

View

- Presentation Views: Normal, Outline, Slide Sorter, Notes Page, Reading View
- Master Views; Slide Master, Handout Master, Notes Master
- Show: Ruler, Gridlines, Guides, Notes
- Zoom: Zoom, Fit to Window
- Color/Grayscale: Show Color, Gray, Black & White
- Window: New Windows, Arrange All, Cascade, Move Split, Switch Windows
- Macros: Use to record new macros or run macros you already have

Format (visible when an object is clicked)

- Insert Shapes: Scroll or dropdown to see complete list of autoshapes; Edit Shape, Text Box
- Shape Styles: Theme Fills, Shape Fill, Shape Outline, Shape Effects
- WordArt Styles: Theme Styles, Text Fill, Text Outline, Text Effects
- Arrange: Front/Back, Align, Group, Rotate
- Size: Width, Height

Remember that the Ribbon changes, depending on where you are. Many options only appear when you are in that specific operation or step. In addition to the "Format" tab (which only appears when you click on an object or text), you also will see tabs for Table Tools (Design, Layout), Picture Tools (Format), Drawing Tools (Format), Chart Tools (Design, Format), and SmartArt Tools (Design, Format).

Screen Shortcuts

Although *all* commands are on the ribbon, certain commands are so frequently used that PowerPoint has shortcuts to get to them. There are two useful sets of shortcuts.

One set of shortcuts is a quick toolbar for formatting text. It includes commonly used formats such as font, size, bold, italic, underline, alignment, color, enlarge/shrink, and indent.

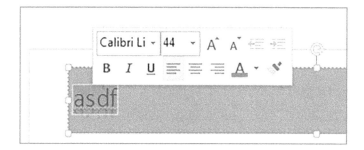

A second set of shortcuts will appear for charts and graphs. There are three buttons that will appear at the right side of the chart:

- Chart Elements: What parts of the chart do you want to include
- Chart Styles: Design and colors
- Chart Filters: Values (data series) to be included or dropped from the display

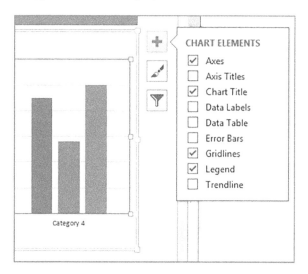

An additional set of shortcuts are located on the right mouse button. The options that appear when you right click are determined by what you are pointing your mouse at *when* you click:

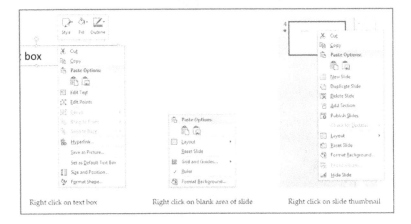

| Right click on text box | Right click on blank area of slide | Right click on slide thumbnail |

You can also use Shift + F10 to pull up the shortcut menu.

Screen Panes

"Screen Panes" appear on the right side of the screen, but only when you click on certain options. For example, if you click on the Design tab and select "Format Background," you'll suddenly get the "Task Pane," with options for how you want to fill your background; if you click on Format/Selection Pane, you'll get a screen for showing or hiding parts of a slide.

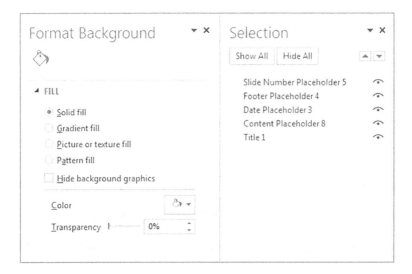

There are panes for many options, including these:

- **Format Background**: Solid fill, gradient fill, picture or text fill, pattern fill, hide background graphics, color, and transparency
- **Animation Pane** (under the Animation tab on the Ribbon): Includes effect options (lines, words, or characters), timing, sound, and more
- **Selection Pane** (under the Format tab): Show or hide elements of each slide
- **Comments Pane** (under Review): Show all comments within the presentation
- **Spell Check** (under Review)
- **Research** (under Review)
- **Thesaurus** (under Review)

Screen panes stay on the screen until you click the X in the corner to close them.

Screen Views

One of the important elements to remember is the set of View buttons at the bottom right corner of the screen. These four buttons determine which "view" you will see on your screen:

- Normal: The "normal" view splits your screen three ways: at the left is the thumbnail view (or outline view, depending on your View Ribbon settings), at the bottom is the notes view, and in the center is the slide
- Slide Sorter: See an overview of all slides. Use the sorter to rearrange your slides and to create the slide show using "transitions" and timing
- Reading View: Removes all the PowerPoint commands and shows a simple version of the slide for reading purposes (not a slide show)
- Slide Show — Run your slide show via a projector or large screen

Most of your work will be done in the Normal view. But there are times — such as when you need to organize your slides — that it becomes more efficient to switch into the Sorter view.

The Slide Show view is doubly important, as it generally takes the place of what most people would do with "Print Preview." There are many features in PowerPoint that you don't really see until you run the show (such as animation effects, dims, timing).

Basic Slide Content

After you choose a layout, you generally have two fundamental types of content: graphics and text.

Images

A graphic can be created from many sources. It may be from clip art (predrawn artwork that can be edited); it can be drawn free hand; it could be scanned in or pasted in from other programs; it can be downloaded from the internet or your camera. Graphics can also be created from a layout (such as for charts and for SmartArt). In addition to drawing tools for creating lines, circles, and arrows, PowerPoint also provides "autoshapes," which draw commonly used shapes such as cubes and hearts, as well as shapes for flow charts, connectors, and "action buttons."

All graphics are controlled by **handles**. Handles are the block-dots that appear in each corner of an image, and in the center between corners (8 per object). Handles are used to control the **size** of the graphic. If you point your mouse at any handle, it turns into a double-edged arrow; the direction the arrow points is the direction in which you can drag (↔↕↖↘). They will stretch the image larger or smaller, longer or shorter, or wider or narrower. However, if you don't want to distort a picture, be sure to stretch from the corner handles *while holding your shift key*. In Power-Point, dragging the corner handles with shift held down preserves the shape. Handles should *not* be used to move or reposition the graphic. If you want to move the graphic to a different location, point in the center and get the four-sided mouse arrow, then click and drag it where you want it.

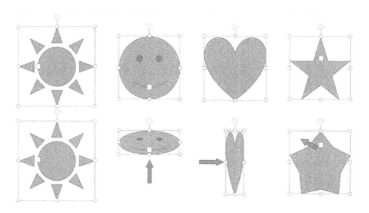

At the top of many types of graphics, you will also see a circular arrow. This is the "rotate" command, to turn your picture at an angle. There may also be a yellow handle somewhere on the image; this is an adjustment handle, and can be used to change the shape. Here is a typical shape, with two adjustments:

If you wish to edit the parts of a graphic (such as clip art), you must turn on each part's handles. For example, if you have a clip art of a woman wearing a blue dress and you want to turn the dress red, you should click the dress handles to avoid turning the entire woman red. To do this, you may first need to break the graphic into its components, a step called "ungroup" (located on the Format tab that appears when you click on a graphic). Once the art is ungrouped, you may have to select ungroup a second time to completely break it apart. Once it is totally ungrouped, you can click on individual parts and make changes. Then, when done, you might want to turn the image back into a group.

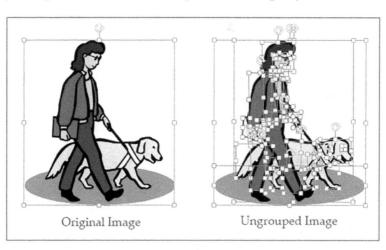

Original Image   Ungrouped Image

Remember: Every element on a slide, whether text or graphic, is controlled by handles.

Text

Text is similar to graphics, but is controlled by a second feature: frames. Frames are the gray borders that surround the text (commonly called "text boxes"). To type within a frame, simply click inside it. To stop typing, click OFF the slide (outside the page), which turns off the frame.

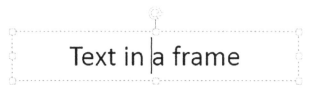

To work with a frame, you must first click in it, which puts your cursor into it for typing; it shows the frame, but the frame is not active (dotted frame). *Clicking the frame again activates the frame handles and removes your cursor from typing mode (solid frame).*

Text in a frame

Like graphics, stretching the frame handles will make the frame larger or smaller; it will not, however, affect the size of the text within the frame (beyond word wrap within the frame). Text size is controlled by format with the Ribbon and the Format tab. But the size of the frame is important, since it controls the size of any box or border you put around the frame or any fill you put into the background of the text.

Unlike graphics, to move a frame and its contents, do not click in the middle; this puts you back into typing mode (editing the text). Instead, click the *frame itself*, and drag the entire border (not just the handles) wherever you want the text to be positioned.

Clicking on a text frame (so there is *no* cursor visible in the text) is the same as highlighting text for formatting. For example, if you click on the frame and turn on underline, all words and spaces within the frame will be underlined. (If you click in the middle of one word, only that word will be underlined; you can also highlight text, just as in word processing, to select parts to format.)

Design Elements of a Slide

In addition to layout, text, and graphics, every slide contains an overall design feature called its "Theme." Themes in PowerPoint consist of four components:

- Color scheme
- Fonts
- Effects
- Background

These are located on the Design tab. They can be changed for the individual slide, or the changes can be made global (the purpose of the slide master). The default is global; you can right-click a theme design to select "apply only to selected slides."

What a theme does is to define a set of slide masters for your presentation (commonly referred to as a "design template"). If you have two or three theme designs you wants to use, you will also have two or three sets of masters. The slide masters are the overall slide formats, containing anything you want on each page (such as page numbers or logos). There are a number of templates and slide masters already built-in to PowerPoint to work with (see below).

Theme Designs and Variants

When you start PowerPoint, your file is automatically set to the theme design called the "Office" theme. This establishes the colors you have to work with, the fonts you type with, the background options you have to choose from, and the effects (such as 3-D or glow) you have to pick from.

Use the Design tab on the Ruler to switch themes. There are 28 other themes built in to PowerPoint (and more can be downloaded from File/New). Note that the automatic setting is that the theme design you select will apply to your entire presentation.

Once you've chosen a theme, you can then select a "variant"—changing the colors, fonts, effects, and background styles. Note that when selecting colors and fonts, you have a "Customize" option. When you customize your colors and fonts, you can save them so that PowerPoint remembers them for future use (one step in your "branding").

Custom themes that you have created can be saved and reused. On the dropdown for the designs is a "Browse" command for finding themes that you have saved (make sure your store them where you can find them again!).

Colors

The color scheme is where you specify the color combinations you wish to use as defaults in your presentation. A color scheme automatically changes all slides in the presentation. It contains 12 colors for the following elements:

- Text/Background Dark (1 and 2)
- Text/Background Light (1 and 2)
- 6 Accents
- Hyperlink
- Followed Hyperlink.

On the Customize Colors menu, you will see the built-in color combinations from the various design themes. At the bottom is the command to "Customize Colors." This way, you can pick your own colors and then save them under a different name so they are remembered for use in other presentations.

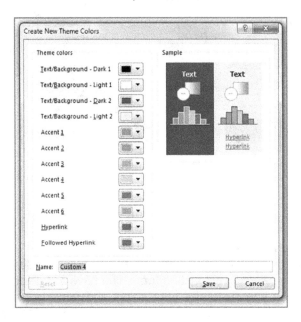

For each slide element, use the dropdown to select a new color. The colors that automatically appear are the current (Office Theme) colors, plus the ten colors that Microsoft calls "Standard." Use the "More Colors" command to find the expanded standard color screen, *plus* the "Custom" color screen.

The Custom Colors operate on the principle of RGB (Red, Green, Blue), part of the light spectrum (or the rainbow colors red, orange, yellow, green, blue, indigo, and violet). Mixing red and green yields orange and yellow; mixing blue and and red yields indigo and violet. The maximum value for the red, green, and blue is 255; if all three are set to 255, you get white; if all three are set to 0, you get black. Here are a few sample colors as an example:

R	128	163	82	0
G	0	0	0	76
B	0	66	99	151
=	UofC maroon	LUC maroon	NWU purple	Fermi Blue

Be sure to watch the "Sample" preview on your screen. Note that the first four colors control the overall slide design.

Fonts

The Design/Fonts dropdown lets you specify two standard fonts for use within the presentation, one for Headings and one for Body (the assumption is you might want your headings to stand out and look different from your content). Again, like Colors, these can be saved for re-use.

Be careful when selecting fonts. Make sure you use easy-to-read fonts (avoid fancy scripts or small type). If you will be sharing the presentation online or over email, you might also want to stay with what are considered the (somewhat) safe fonts to share between PCs and Macs:

Arial	Times New Roman
Arial Italic	*Times New Roman Italic*
Arial Bold	**Times New Bold**
Arial Bold Italic	***Times New Bold Italic***
Arial Black	Trebuchet MS
Arial Unicode	*Trebuchet MS Italic*
Comic Sans MS	**Trebuchet MS Bold**
Comic Sans MS Bold	***Trebuchet MS Bold Italic***
Georgia	Verdana
Georgia Italic	*Verdana Italic*
Georgia Bold	**Verdana Bold**
Georgia Bold Italic	***Verdana Bold Italic***

Fonts available on both Mac OS X and Windows

Effects

These are built-in combination of special effects that impact objects on your slides. The theme choices control how features such as Shadow, Reflection, Glow, Soft Edges, Bevel, and 3-D Rotation are applied within your presentation. (These choices can be individually controlled on the Format ribbon.)

Background Styles

Slide backgrounds make a slide easier for your audience to view. Think carefully about what would make an appropriate background, and how to use it creatively on different slides. A general rule is to use dark backgrounds in dark rooms and light backgrounds in light rooms (in a dark room, what's light, i.e., your content, is what should stand out; reverse the logic for bright rooms). If you want to really stand out, avoid commonly used colors like blue, white, and gray.

There are five kinds of backgrounds you can apply in PowerPoint. There are dozens of built-in designs and variations found on the Design tab, but there is also an option for creating your own background style. That is where you will find settings for:

- Solid fill—pick a color
- Gradient fill—shades based on either preset designs or gradients you create:
  o Type (linear, radial, rectangular, on a path, from the title)
  o Direction (top to bottom, left to right)
  o Angle (in degrees)
  o Gradient stops (where you specify how many colors you want to use, i.e., 3 colors would mean 3 stops, and how to allocate their location via the "stop position")
  o Position (on the slide)
  o Transparency (from solid 0% to clear 100%)
  o Brightness (from -100% black to +100% white)
- Picture or texture fill (selecting a pre-designed texture, such as marble, or selecting a picture from a file)
- Pattern fill (two colors used to make geometric patterns, such as checks or stripes)
- Hide background graphics (to turn off the background on any given slide)

Note there are two ways to use the background. Selecting a background and hitting the "Close" (X) applies it only to the slide you are currently on. However, at the bottom of the pane is the command to "Apply to All," which formats the entire presentation consistently.

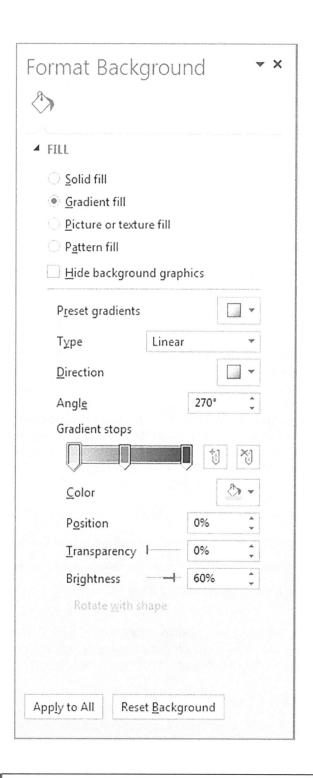

Working with Slides

When you open PowerPoint, you are prompted to select a theme design to work from. The default is the blank presentation. If you click on that, PowerPoint opens a new file, with one slide (a Title page).

Then you must select a layout. PowerPoint assumes you intend to start with a Title slide (although you don't have to; there is a button on the ribbon called "Layout," which lets you switch to any of the layouts available in your file).

Title Slide

The Title slide layout has two parts for typing: an area for the title, and an area for the subtitle. Simply point at the title area or subtitle area with the mouse, click, and type your text. To indicate you are done typing, click out of the box (or off the page) to remove your cursor; if you need to change text once it has been inserted, point at where you wish the change to be, click (be sure you see the I-bar), and use delete (right-delete) or backspace (left-delete) to remove text. Then type in the new content.

To put text somewhere other than in a title or subtitle on the page, use the Shapes dropdown on the Drawing ribbon and use the A-tool (text box). To move text, click on the grid around the text, then pull it wherever you want it on the page. Use the handles to adjust size, width, and height.

Remember: To format all the text within a box, click on the outline of the box (turn on the handles). To format *part* of the text within a box, highlight the part you wish to change, or click in the middle of a word if you only want to change one word.

Once you are finished typing your content into your first slide, use the "New Slide" button's dropdown to select your second slide layout. Don't forget every now and then to click "save."

Title and Content Slide

Use the "New Slide" button on the Slides ribbon to insert a new slide (do not confuse "new slide" with "new file"). If you click the

New Slide button, the default is a layout called "Title and Content." This layout can be used to create either a bulleted list or content controlled by the buttons in the center, each representing a different kind of content:

- Table
- Chart
- SmartArt
- Pictures (from your computer)
- Pictures (from online, including clipart)
- Video

Each of these is discussed below.

Bullet Slide

To do a bulleted list, you just click where it says "Click to add text." This starts the bullet process. Use the bullet dropdown on the Paragraph group of the Home ribbon to adjust and format your bullets. The dropdown allows you to choose other bullets (such as Wingdings and Webdings, or picture bullets), change their color, and adjust their size. Use the tab key on your keyboard or the "Increase Indent" on the ribbon to lower the level of each bullet. Use shift-tab or "Decrease Indent" to raise the level of each bullet (Increase and Decrease are Paragraph buttons on the ribbon).

When using buttons, you might want to consider applying an animation (see below for more details about animations) to your list. If you do, look under Effect Options in the Animation pane, where you'll find a command called "Dim." This makes your bullet lines turn a different color during the presentation. As each new item appears, the previous items can be faded to a different color you determine.

Table Slide

Using the same "Title and Content" slide layout, the first button in the center is called "Insert Table." When you click it, a dialog window appears, asking you to define the number of columns and number of rows you want in your table. (You can easily change this with the Ribbon if you find you need more or less.)

Click OK to position the table on the slide. You'll find a new set of tabs on the Ribbon called "Table Tools". The Design tab contains style options, preformatted table styles, and border and fill options.

The Layout tab is very important. It allows you to insert and delete columns and rows, merge and split cells, and control size and alignment.

As you type into your table, you can use the Tab key on the keyboard to move from cell to cell. When you reach the last cell, if you tab again, PowerPoint starts a new row.

Chart (Graph) Slide

Again using the "Title and Content" layout, click the second button to create a graphic chart. A popup window appears, asking you to select a chart type to insert (column, line, pie, bar, area, etc.).

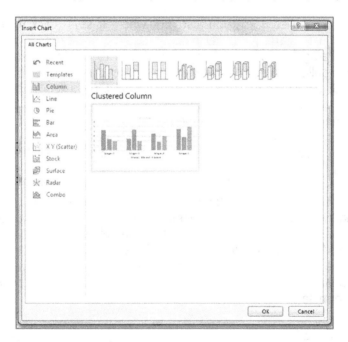

Once you select a chart type, a simple spreadsheet (Excel) appears, laid out for inserting your data to generate a chart. It defaults to 3 columns of data (Series) and 4 rows (Category). If you need more or less, grab the corner of the blue outline around the data and stretch to the desired size.

When you have finished entering your data, hit the "X" to close the spreadsheet. This returns you to PowerPoint, where the chart can now be edited and formatted.

Once you're back on the chart, you'll see a new set of tabs (called "Chart Tools") on the ribbon:

- *Design* lets you change the chart type, switch rows and columns, edit the data (in Excel), and format the chart with various chart styles. At the very beginning is a key button called "Add Chart Element," which lets you add additional components to a chart (such as axes labels).
- *Format* provides graphical styles (such as fills, outlines, and effects) and text styles (WordArt styles). At the beginning is a dropdown which lets you see all the areas of a chart which can be formatted.

You can also right-click any part of the chart to get formatting options or edit the data, or use the three buttons down the right side for shortcuts in formatting.

SmartArt Slide

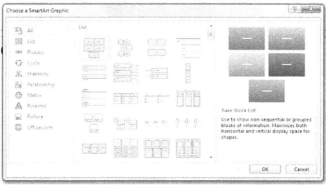

The third button brings up SmartArt. A popup window appears, asking you to choose the kind of SmartArt Graphic you would like:

- List
- Process
- Cycle
- Hierarchy
- Relationship
- Matrix
- Pyramid

- Picture
- More Online at Office.com

SmartArt provides a way to present information visually, rather than relying on lists or bullets. It also presents hierarchical and cyclical designs (such as organization charts and Venn diagrams). See the section on SmartArt on page 32 for more details.

SmartArt Organizational Chart

Organizational charts are located in the Hierarchy category of SmartArt. In addition to the slide title, there are automatic text boxes for

- Head
- Assistant
- Subordinates (default is 3).

On the new tabs, the first button is "Add Shape," which allows you to select any box in the chart, then add another box above it, below it, or on either side. Under Layouts are different ways to arrange your boxes, and SmartArt Styles provide effects and colors.

Using Photographs on a Slide

On the "Title and Content" layout, the 4th and 5th buttons insert picture—either from a file, or from online photos and clip art.

To insert a photograph from a file, it must be stored on some disk (hard disk, CD, USB). You must navigate to where it is stored, find it, then select it and hit "insert" to put it on the slide.

There are alternative ways to bring photographs into PowerPoint. One is to use the slide layout called "Picture with Caption." This is very handy if you want your pictures consistently sized.

An additional way to bring in a picture is to use the Insert tab on the ribbon, which gives you an option to start a "Photo Album," which is a collection of pictures.

Yet *another* way to bring images into a slide is to use the "Screen-shot" button on the Insert tab of the Ribbon. This dropdown allows you to insert a screen capture from an already-open window, or insert a "screen clip" — a portion (cropped area) of a screen you would like to insert.

The screen clip command works only on the *most recently opened* window. To use it, first open the screen you want to capture. Then go to your PowerPoint slide and click on the dropdown for Screen-shot, then click on Screen Clipping. You will be moved back to the previous window; pause for a second until it fades out, then use the mouse to drag a box around the portion you want to use. When you release the mouse button, the screen capture is in-serted on your slide.

Once the picture is on the slide, you can use the handles to control its size (remember to always use the Shift key and corner handles if you don't want to mess up its shape). The Picture Tools tab on the ribbon gives you options to format the picture, including changing the shape, adding reflections, recoloring, creating bor-ders and effects, sizing, and cropping (cutting off portions you don't want to see).

Using Online Clip Art on a Slide

The fifth button opens an online search window. You must specify a "keyword" that PowerPoint will match with both photographs and clipart. Note there is range of plates where you can search (only one at a time); Office.com, Bing (web search), and OneDrive (cloud search). When the search is finished, the matching images are displayed in the search window.

Images frequently need to be re-sized, but most clip art does not enlarge well (definition is lost, image becomes grainy or fuzzy). Photographs can be sized larger or smaller, usually with minimal change in quality.

To edit clip art in PowerPoint, such as changing the colors, you must first use the "Ungroup" button under "Home/Arrange" to break the picture into its individual components. Then each part can be changed (right-click to "edit points"), formatted, or deleted. (You cannot ungroup or edit parts of a photograph or scanned object in PowerPoint; you must use a photo editor such as Adobe PhotoShop if you wish to edit that kind of graphic; PowerPoint *does* allow some minor changes to a photo, through the use of the "picture" toolbar; with it, you can crop, lighten/darken, change contrast, recolor, apply filters, and watermark a photograph.)

Note: To re-group an item, draw a line around it with your mouse ("marquee" or lasso), so that all handles are turned on. Then use the "Group" button to turn it back into a unit.

Sometimes you want to have graphics on a slide, but you don't want the graphical layout. An additional way to bring in clip art and pictures is to use the Insert tab on the Ribbon. This gives you the same options, but it just drops the items onto the slide, where you can then size and position them wherever you lie.

Using Video on a Slide

The last button on the "Title and Content" layout is video. Clicking it brings up a window called "Insert Video." PowerPoint looks for videos in the following locations (one at a time):

- From a file (browse) on your computer
- OneDrive (browse the cloud)
- YouTube (search YouTube)
- Video Embed Code (cut and paste an embedded code, such as from Vimeo)
- Facebook

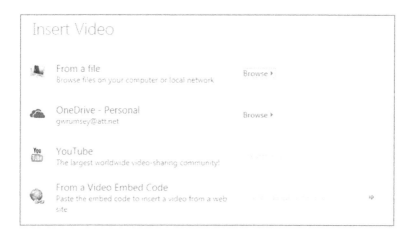

When you select and insert the media clip, you find a new section on the Ribbon for "Video Tools." There are two tabs:

- Format: Play, Adjust, Video Styles and Effects (such as, play in a shape like a circle rather than a rectangle)
- Playback: Play, Fade, Volume, Start (on click, or automatically), Hide (while not playing), Rewind

Other Slide Layouts

Other slide layouts include
- Section Header—divide your presentation into sections
- Two Content—side-by-side content areas, so you could add combinations of bullets and pictures, or charts and clip art, etc.
- Comparison
- Title Only—a text box for the title, but rest of slide is empty
- Blank—empty, so you can add whatever you would like
- Content with Caption
- Picture with Caption

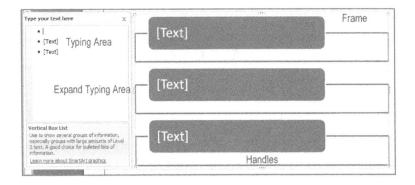

SmartArt

SmartArt is a way to present information in a visually appealing way, without resorting to bland bullets or boring lists. It works consistently across Word, Excel, and PowerPoint. You begin by using the Insert tab on the Ribbon, where you find SmartArt listed in the Illustrations group. Clicking it brings up a selection of SmartArt types, including List, Process, Cycle, Hierarchy, Relationship, Matrix, and Pyramid, each with a variety of formats. Select one to insert the SmartArt skeleton into your document. This automatically adds two new tabs to the ribbon: Design and Format.

At the left of the SmartArt is a text-typing area which can be closed (X in the corner) or opened (double-arrows on frame). Press enter to create a new level; press Tab to indent or create a sub-bullet. When formatting and designing, note that many of the selections can be "previewed" by pointing your mouse at the option (but don't click).

Manipulating SmartArt

Selecting: To manipulate a SmartArt object, you first select or highlight it. To do this, simply place your pointer anywhere in the graphic and click once. Graphical "handles" should appear on the edges.

Moving: With the object active, point the mouse at the frame or border outlining the graphic, then click and drag, moving the mouse, and the chart moves with you.

Resizing: To enlarge, shrink or change the shape of the object, place the pointer on any of the "handles" on the frame until the pointer's shape changes into double-arrows, then click and drag. The outline you draw will change the chart accordingly. Corner handles enlarge and shrink.

Many of the components of a SmartArt object also have handles, which can be stretched and pulled to re-size that part of the graphic.

Formatting: Clicking once on a SmartArt object will allow you to move it or change its dimensions. But you may want to change other aspects as well. One option is to click once on any specific part of the chart, then right-click with your mouse to find "change" and "format" options. Alternatively, you can use the ribbon tabs, as explained below. Remember to click the Home tab for simple formats (font, size, center, color).

Deselecting: After completing your changes, simply "Click Away" – click any where in the document outside the object.

Design

Create Graphic

Add Shape — Opens the dialog window that allows you to select the kind of chart you wish to have (column, line, pie, bar, area, XY, stock, surface, doughnut, bubble, radar). There are multiple designs for each chart type; for example, for column charts, there are side-by-side, stacked, percentile, and front-to-back.

Add Bullet — Adds either another entry of the same level within the hierarchy, or a sublevel.

Right to Left — Aligns content on the right instead of the left.

Layout — Saves an edited chart as a template, so it can be re-used.

Promote/Demote — Indents and unindents bullets and levels (same as Tab and Shift-Tab). Turns a main level entry into a subentry, or a subentry into a main entry.

Text Pane — Activates the text-typing box.

Layouts

This option allows you to switch from one SmartArt design into a different one, for example, from 3 horizontal boxes to 3 vertical boxes or to a pyramid.

SmartArt Styles

Change Colors — Select new color combinations (based on Theme colors) for the content.

Effects — Various designs you can select to create 3-dimensional or shaded effects (note this is one of the features where you can preview by pointing your mouse at an option without clicking).

Reset

Cancels any formatting changes you have made and restores the SmartArt object to the original format.

Format

Shapes

Impacts the shapes within a SmartArt object. You can change the shape (switch a box to an arrow), or make the shape larger or smaller.

Shape Styles

Predesigned or custom fills, outlines, and effects for the components of the graphic (such as fill colors or borders or shadows).

Word Art Styles

Predesigned or custom text formats, including text fill (color), text outline (border), and text effects (such as glow).

Arrange

Bring to front or send to back (used when there are multiple objects embedded within a chart.

Size

The horizontal and vertical dimensions of your chart. This is an alternative way of sizing, as opposed to dragging handles. (Note that the dropdown in the corner provides a "Format Shape" pane, which has a checkbox for "Lock aspect ratio," which will keep the dimensions consistent.)

Animations

The Animations tab on the ribbon controls individual elements on the slide (based on handles). (Don't confuse it with "transitions," which is how the slide itself appears.) Any part of your slide can have animations, which can control the following "effects":

- Entrance—how it appears on the slide during the presentation
- Emphasis—what happens to it once it is on the slide
- Exit—how it should disappear from the slide when no longer needed
- Motion Path—make it move around on a path that you draw.

Use the dropdown for "Add Animation" to see your choices. Use one of the "More" options at the bottom if you would like to see the full range of options *and* preview the choices before selecting one.

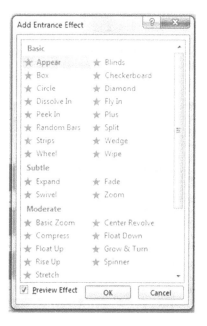

Once an animation has been selected, there will be new options for when it should start (on click or automatically), how fast or slow, and long before it starts. There is also the "Animation Pane," which gives you more options (including "remove" the effect if you don't like it), as well as choices to "Modify" the effect (start, direction, and speed).

The animation effect itself will be shown as a numbered list, based on its sequence in the show. You can drag the numbered items up and down to change the sequence. When you click on a numbered item, you also will find that it is highlighted in the Animation Pane, so you can manipulate it. The clicked numbered item in the Animation Pane has a dropdown, for "Effect Options" (which includes sound effects and dimming) and "Timing."

Transitions

Transitions control how the overall slide appears in the course of the presentation. The choices are located on the Transitions tab on the Ribbon.

There are many transitions built into PowerPoint, such as fade, push, checkerboard, split, and dissolve, located on the "Transition" dropdown; there are also a lot of wacky and institutional designs, like honeycomb, glitter, ripple, and vortex.

The toolbar gives you buttons to control the speed of the transition (most seem to look more interesting if they are slowed down a bit) and sound. There is a button called "Apply to All," which makes all slides use the same settings, for consistency in your presentation.

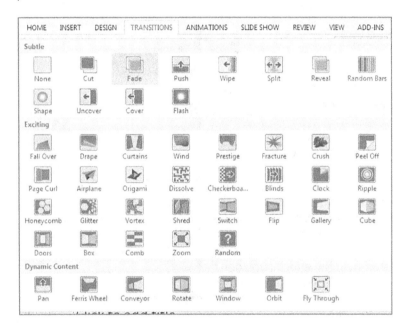

Speaker Notes

Speaker notes are shown at the bottom of each slide, and the available work space can be expanded by stretching the bar at the top of the notes area. A more complete view is gained by going to the View tab on the ribbon and clicking "Notes Page." Clicking on this brings up a screen where you see your slide on the top half of the page and any notes you want to type on the bottom half. Once you've finished typing the notes, click on the "Normal" View button to return to the regular view.

The purpose of speaker notes is to print them out to have in front of you during your presentation. To print the speaker's notes, go to "File" and select "Print." There you will find an option that shows "Full Page Slides," but which has a dropdown, with options to print the actual slides, the handouts, the speaker notes, or the outline. This same dropdown also has options to control the print quality and to frame the slides (put a border around them when they print).

Printing Handouts

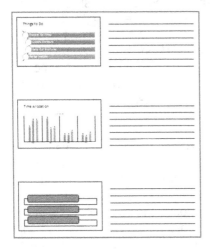

Handouts are small versions of your slides, printed multiples to a page (often referred to as "thumbnails"). You can then use them to pass out to your audience so they can keep track of the presentation and take notes. Be sure to select how many you want per page: 1 per page, 2, 3 (with lines for taking notes), 4, or more.

Also on the print screen are options to print in black and white (rather than gray scale or color), to choose which slide(s) to print, to size the slide to fit the page (scale), and to switch printers and settings. Note that on gray-scale printers (such as laser printers), frequently the "Color" option prints better than the grayscale or black and white options (which substitute shades for colors, resulting in poor print readability).

There are also options to "frame slides" (put a border around them on the printed page), and to print "high quality" (more ink!).

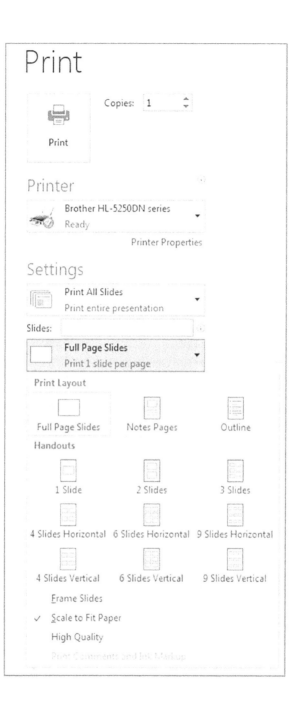

Using the Outline View

The outline view gives you quick access to text without having to worry about graphics. The Outline screen is useful for text editing, spell checking, and similar text-oriented functions. It is not particularly helpful for formatting.

In the Outline View (use the View tab on the Ribbon to turn on Outline View), each time you hit the "Enter" or return key on the keyboard, you start a new slide. If you are not trying to create a new slide but instead want to add text to your current slide, use the tab key after you hit enter; this converts the new slide into content on the current slide.

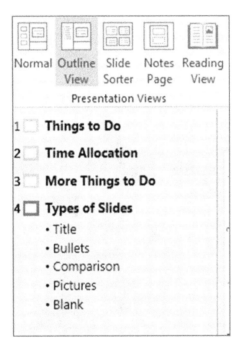

Using the Slide Sorter

The sorter (the second button at bottom right, or View/Slide Sorter) gives you an overview of all slides in the presentation. To rearrange a slide's order, click and drag it to where you want it to be. Use "Copy" and "Paste" to duplicate a slide in order to use it over again (such as repeating a cover at the end of the presentation).

Users often find the Sorter helpful for setting up their slide show. You can get an overview of how one slide transitions to another, and decide how to allocate time for each slide.

In this illustration, the sorter is being used in conjunction with the Slide Show tab of the Ribbon, so that timing can be applied to each slide for an automatically running presentation. The Rehearse Timings command adds a clock to your screen presentation for testing various time limits, and the Record Slide Show lets you include narration (and laser pointing) if you have a microphone in your computer (see the following section for more detail).

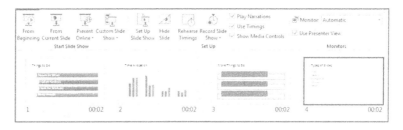

Creating a Slide Show

A slide show consists of all or part of your slides strung together into a presentation, much like a movie. Each slide has its "transition," which tells PowerPoint how to make it appear on the screen. Then the "animations" control how the content appears. Finally, you can then specify whether the slide should be on your screen for a given period of time, or whether it should move off when you click the mouse.

On the Slide Show tab of the ribbon are the commands to run or edit the slide show. "Set Up Slide Show" allows you to turn on or off timing, and make the presentation loop repeatedly until you press Escape to make it stop (useful for what is called "kiosk" presentations).

There is also a very useful button called "Hide Slide." This allows you to drop individual slides form a particular presentation without having to delete them from the file. They can be unhidden at any point.

The next buttons are for timing. "Rehearse Timing" records the number of seconds you want a slide to be on-screen, based on a sample run-through. When you click this button, a clock appears in the corner of your screen and your slide show starts. As you click your way through the show (by clicking anywhere on the slides), the clock shows how many seconds the slide has appeared. When the last slide is reached, PowerPoint shows you how many seconds the total show lasts and asks if you would like to use these settings. Clicking "Yes" stores the time next to each slide; to change one slide's time without having to run the timer again for the entire show, use the "Slide Transition" button to record a timing manually.

Viewing the Slide Show

The slide viewer is the fourth button on the bottom right of the screen (or F5 on the keyboard). Once you have built your slides into a show, use the viewer to look at it or project it.

When in the "Slide Show" view, notice the lower left corner of your screen has a small, faint toolbar (jiggle your mouse if you don't see it). You will find useful presentation commands:

- Move forward or backward through your slides
- Turn your pointer into a laser pointer, pen, highlighter, or eraser to remove any "ink"
- Switch to "See all slides" (for navigating)
- Zoom in on part of your slide (Esc to zoom out)
- Black screen/White screen/Presenter view

The "Presenter View" (below) is one of the new additions to PowerPoint 2013. It allows you to see your speaker notes, your next slide, your current slide, *and* have the zoom/pointer toolbar — all on your screen simultaneously, while your audience only see the presentation. But be warned, it takes a lot of practice to master.

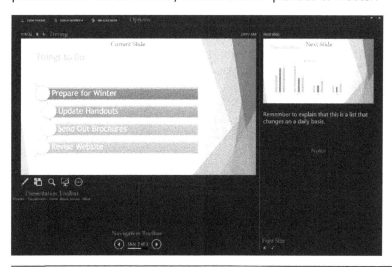

Other Presentation Options

PowerPoint also comes with a "run-time viewer," which can be copied to a disk and used to run your presentation on any computer (even if PowerPoint is not on that computer). Look under the File tab on the Ribbon and select "Export," where you will find an extremely useful command called "Package Presentation for CD" (although CD can also mean a Flash USB drive, if you use the button "Copy to Folder").

"Package for CD" is also useful because it collects all your embedded files and makes sure they are all on the disk as well. Embedded files include fonts, media clips, graphs, and anything else that came from outside of PowerPoint.

On the Options mean of Package you will find the choices to include linked files, embed your fonts, and add a password for security.

Also under File/Export are commands to export to PDF, video formats, and other options. Just above Export on the File menu is "Share," which allows you to save it to OneDrive (the Microsoft cloud that comes with 2013), and then invite people to see it or work on it, or email it to people, or even run a presentation online (assuming you use Microsoft Lync).

Templates

There are numerous design formats already built into PowerPoint. When you begin a new presentation, PowerPoint allows you to pick from one of the existing templates instead of having to start a blank presentation (see the Design tab on the ribbon). These templates have colors, designs, fonts, and formats already in place, so you only have to type in your information. They can all be edited.

More templates can be download into PowerPoint, by going to File/New and clicking on the search bar (based on keyword searching). The results may be a wide variety of PowerPoint formats, not just presentations, and some may be one page of design while others may have multiple pages of design and content.

To apply a design to a currently existing file, first open the file, then click on the Design tab on the ribbon. Under the Themes dropdown is an option to browse for more themes. Use that to find the designs you have saved, and select the one you wish to use. That will pull its design, background, colors, fonts, and effects into your current PowerPoint file.

What many PowerPoint users never discover is that templates are simply "master pages" (see below) that have been set up and saved for re-use. To create your own templates, design using your presentation's master pages — not the slides. Then you can go to "Save As" and change the file type from "Presentation" (.pptx) to "Design template" (.potx). Notice that the folder location automatically changes to the templates location; templates *must* be saved in the template folder. Then, remember never to open—that puts you back in the original template.

The point of a template is to be able to re-use it, time and again. So, to use a template properly, always click on "New" file, which starts the template window. Then click on Custom/Custom Office Templates, and you'll see the list of templates you have on your computer. Double-click the one you want to use, and you will have a *new presentation* to work with (*not* the template). Many people try to do this with the "Save as" command—but that's not a template!

Slide Masters

Ultimately, Slide Masters are the key to becoming an efficient and effective PowerPoint user. Slide Masters allow you to make global changes and format with global consistency.

Every PowerPoint file has a set of slide masters (found under "View/Slide Master" on the Ribbon) where you can edit the title and text formats (fonts, size, color, fill, etc.). Any changes made on the master automatically show up on all slides in the presentation. This is where you put in headers and footers, dates, names, logos, or other elements you would like to appear on each slide (you can always go back to the Design tab and check the box to "Hide Background Graphics" from any one slide, without affecting the masters).

In PowerPoint, there are master slides for each layout you can use (you will also find that different template designs have different kinds and numbers of layouts, so your masters will look different). Changing any one master layout changes all the slides that use that layout (i.e., changing the Title and Content master will update all your slides that have the Title and Content layout; change the bullets on your master, all your bullets throughout your presentation will change).

When you go to View/Slide Master, you switch from your presentation view to your Master view. The key part is down the left side of the screen, where you see a variety of slide layouts. Each layout controls one of the layouts listed on the "New Slide" button. At the top of the master slide thumbnails is the large Master Master. Changing the Master Master changes all the other layout masters, so this is where you begin. Note that the Ribbon has changed to display key concepts talked about in this handout, including themes, colors, fonts, effects, and backgrounds. You can also go to Insert and set up headers and footers (with automatic date, name, and slide number).

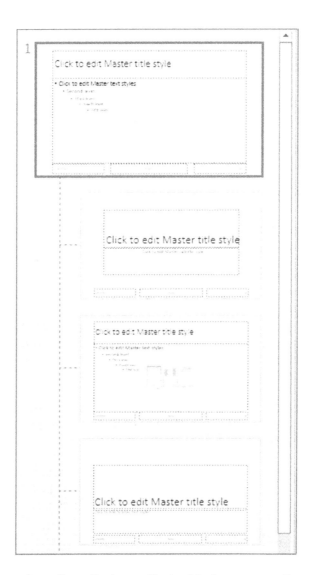

Once you have formatted your Master Master, you can then go to each layout Master and make additional format decisions. For example, you might want your title slide to be a little fancier than your content slides (perhaps a more elaborate background), so go to the first smaller slide Master below the Master Master and make your changes—all title slides in your handout will be reformatted automatically. Go to the second small Master and change your bullets, and all your Title and Content slides will be reformatted. (If for some reason, such as they were manually formatted *not using* the masters, there is a Reset button on your Home Ribbon.)

There are two additional important concepts about masters:

1. You can create additional Master layouts—you aren't limited to the ones that show up initially. If there are particular slide layouts you find useful, use the "Insert Layout" button on the Ribbon to create a new layout, then use the additional buttons for Insert Placeholder, Title, Footers to design it.

2. You can create more Master Masters. Suppose two people are giving a joint presentation. But she wants green for her content, and he wants blue for his content. How do you get two different designs in the same presentation, without having to do each slide individually? It's very easy if you create a second Master Master, by using the "Insert Slide Master" button. This creates a second Master Master, with its own series of layouts, which can be formatted separately from the other Master Master layouts, including having a different theme. You can create as many Master Masters as you need to hold various designs.

Note that if you try to use two or three separate designs (from the Design tab) within the same presentation, you will automatically be generating multiple Master Masters.

In addition to Slide Masters, there are also master views for handouts and notes pages. This can be useful for putting in your own content (such as name, telephone, email) on your handouts and notes.

Useful PowerPoint Shortcuts

- Spell Check as You Type—The redline squiggle under words indicates that a word is not in the dictionary, and may be misspelled. To correct it or add it to the dictionary, right click it with the mouse. Blue lines indicate grammar questions.
- Under Tools/AutoCorrect, you can store frequently typed words and phrases under shortcuts. For example, xxx could insert Chicago, Illinois.
- Under Review, "New Comment" puts a 'note-it' on your slide—sticky notes. They can be useful when more than one person is working on the slide.
- All the standard Ctrl-key shortcuts that work in Word and Excel (such as Ctrl-S to save or Ctrl-Z to undo or Ctrl-X, C, V for Cut/Copy and Paste) work in PowerPoint.
- One useful keystroke is F2, which is a toggle for text fields between type-mode for editing and frame-mode for formatting and moving. Don't forget you can also use your arrow keys to position objects on the slide, rather than the mouse.
- Another useful keystroke is F5, which launches the presentation/slide show. You can use your keyboard to move through it, with keys such as the arrow keys or Page Up/Page Down to go forward or backward.
- On the Home tab under the Drawing section is an option for "Arrange." This features gives you options for automatically lining up objects on a slide, or positioning items correctly on the slide (such as center and middle); it also has an evenly distribute command to spread them out equally.
- "Arrange" also gives you a feature called "gridlines and guides." "Snap objects to grid" is the annoying feature that sometimes prevents you from aligning an object exactly where you want it to go—it jumps up or down or over, just a little, and you cannot position it closer (unless you turn off snap objects). "Guides" are on-screen guidelines that can be moved and positioned to help you achieve consistency across slides (for example, so that your titles always start in the same position). Hold your control key and drag a guide to create multiple guides. (These features can also be turned on or off on the View Ribbon.)

- Also on the View tab is a checkbox for "Ruler." The ruler is very useful for controlling the position and distance for bullets and numbering. It works like the ruler in Microsoft Word.
- Any time you have multiple objects on the page that you wish to select (but there are others you *don't* want to include), use the "Lasso" command on your mouse. Point in a blank spot, and pretend you are drawing a box (over and down); this drags a dotted line on your screen. Anything completely enclosed by the dotted line will be selected.
- Remember to use your Shift key when dragging handles to size objects; it keeps shapes from distorting.

Keystroke Shortcuts

One set of keystroke shortcuts are located on the Alt key. Alt takes you to the Ribbon, and gives you a letter or number for each option. For example, Alt, then N, then P takes you to the Ribbon, Insert tab, Pictures command.

A different set of keystrokes are located on the Ctrl key, in combination with other keys on your keyboard. Among the many available, these seem to be the most useful:

Ctrl +

A	Select All
B	Bold
C	Copy
E	Center
F	Find
H	Replace
I	Italic
J	Justify
K	Insert Hyperlink
L	Flush Left
M	New Slide
N	New File
O	Open File
P	Print
Q	Close (Quit)
R	Flush Right
S	Save
T	Font

U	Underline
V	Paste
X	Cut
Y	Repeat/Redo
Z	Undo
Space	Clear Formatting
Delete	Delete one word

Other shortcuts are available on other key combinations, such as:

Ctrl + Shift + >	Increase Font Size
Ctrl + Shift + <	Decrease Font Size
Alt + F9	Show/Hide Guides
Shift+F10	Shortcut Menu
Shift+Enter	Line Break (New Line)

F1	Help
F2	Select Frame/Select or Edit Text
F5	Run Slide Show/Presentation
F6	Move from Pane to Next Pane
F7	Spell Check